W9-AGC-324

Missa Festiva

Festival Mass

(SATB, accompanied)

Music by
JOHN LEAVITT

CHORAL MUSIC
OF

KYRIE

Kyrie eleison, (Alleluia)
Christe eleison,
Kyrie eleison. (Alleluia)

Lord have mercy, (Alleluia)
Christ have mercy,
Lord have mercy. (Alleluia)

GLORIA

Gloria in excelsis Deo.
Et in terra pax
hominibus bonae voluntatis.
Laudamus te. Benedicimus te.
Adoramus te. Glorificamus te.
Gratias agimus tibi
propter magnam gloriam tuam.

Glory to God in the highest.
And on earth peace
to men of goodwill.
We praise you. We bless you.
We adore you. We glorify you.
We give thanks to you
because of your great glory.

CREDO

Credo in unum Deum,
Patrem omnipotentem,
factorem coeli et terrae,
Et in unum Dominum Jesum Christum,
Filium Dei unigenitum.
Et in Spiritum Sanctum
Dominum, et vivificantem.

I believe in one God,
The Father Almighty,
maker of heaven and earth,
And I believe in one Lord Jesus Christ,
the only begotten Son of God,
And I believe in the Holy Spirit,
the Lord and giver of life.

SANCTUS

Sanctus, Sanctus, Sanctus,
Dominus Deus Sabaoth.
Hosanna Deo, Hosanna in excelsis.
Benedictus qui venit
in nomine Domini Dei.
Pleni sunt coeli et terra
gloria tua.

Holy, Holy, Holy,
Lord God of Hosts.
Hosanna to God, Hosanna in the highest.
Blessed is He who comes
in the name of the Lord God.
Heaven and earth are full
of your glory.

AGNUS DEI

Agnus Dei,
qui tollis peccata mundi:
miserere nobis.
Agnus Dei,
qui tollis peccata mundi:
miserere nobis.
Agnus Dei,
qui tollis peccata mundi:
dona nobis pacem. Amen.

Lamb of God,
who takes away the sins of the world,
have mercy upon us.
Lamb of God,
who takes away the sins of the world,
have mercy upon us.
Lamb of God,
who takes away the sins of the world,
grant us peace. Amen.

Missa Festiva

Festival Mass
by
John Leavitt

Missa Festiva was begun in 1988 with the commission of a festival piece for the International Choral Symposium in Kansas City, Missouri. The Sanctus (Festival Sanctus) of this mass was the result of that commission. Other parts of the ordinary followed, the Kyrie & Agnus Dei. The Gloria was finished in the fall of 1990. The Credo, the centerpiece of the mass, weds the work together and was completed in the Spring of 1991, While this work does not purport to be a liturgical mass, it uses texts from the ordinary, sometimes unaltered, sometimes altered to conscribe to musical considerations. These Latin texts, time honored through many centuries, are embraced for their richness as well as a vehicle for excellent choral singing. *Missa Festiva* combines lyrical melody, touches of counterpoint, and an often brilliant piano accompaniment in this first setting of the mass by composer, John Leavitt.

ALSO AVAILABLE:
Optional Chamber Orchestra Score and Parts (SV9149A)
(on Rental Only)

Single Octavos

KYRIE	SATB (SV8904)
KYRIE	SAB (SV8905)
KYRIE	SSA (SV8906)
GLORIA	SATB (SV9116)
FESTIVAL SANCTUS	SATB (SV8821)
AGNUS DEI	SATB (SV9007)
AGNUS DEI	SSA (SV9008)
AGNUS DEI	SAB (SV9009)

KYRIE

Music by
JOHN LEAVITT

SV9149

for the 1991 Choir Showcase Festival, Western Illinois University,
Macomb, IL., James C. Stegall, director

GLORIA

Music by
JOHN LEAVITT

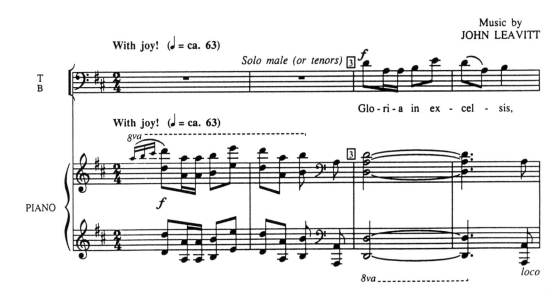

*To be sung: *glo - (o) - ri - a*

14

*To be sung: *pro - (o) - (o) - pter*

CREDO

Music by
JOHN LEAVITT

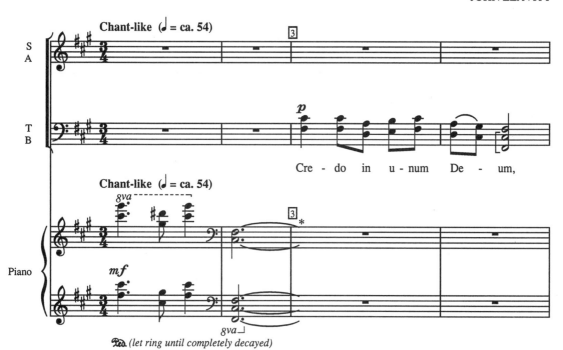

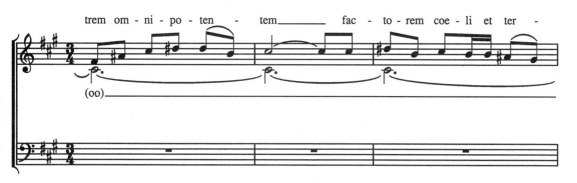

*Piano may double vocal parts for rehearsal only.

*or small ensemble, if needed.

Written for the 1988 International Choral Symposium,
University of Missouri-Kansas City, Dr. Eph Ehly, Director

FESTIVAL SANCTUS

Music by
JOHN LEAVITT

SV9149

for the Liberty, Missouri Senior High Concert Choir, Debra Burnett, director
Missouri Music Educators Association Convention, 1990

AGNUS DEI

Music by
JOHN LEAVITT

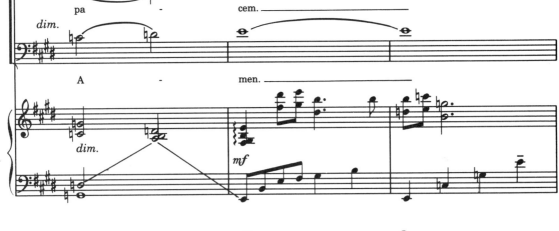